What do you get when you combine Jordan with $O_2$?

(An oxymoron!!)

What's brown and sticky?

(A stick.)

j540.76   Brown, Jordan.
BRO
          Crazy concoctions.

Albert; so close.

$14.95   Grades 3-4   05/11/2012

| DATE | | | |
|---|---|---|---|
| | | | |
| | | | |
| | | | |
| | | | |
| | | | |
| | | | |
| | | | |
| | | | |
| | | | |
| | | | |
| | | | |

Ways to Ge

✓• Mess up

 • Dye his

 • Spread

decode this!
EWXGF   ZQZZZ   UWR

Gravity is a

has three erors.

Time Flies like an arrow. Fruit Flies like a banana.

emories, Jordan!!

What do you get when you combine Jordan with $O_2$?

(An oxymoron!!)

What's brown and sticky?
(A stick.)

$E=MC^{2}3$

So close, Albert; so close.

Ways to Get Revenge on Jordan
✓ • Mess up his precious book.
  • Dye his hair purple.
  • Spread vicious rumors about his singing.

Jordan, decode this!
ASJGF   EWXGF   ZQZZZ   UWR

Gravity is a real downer!

This sentense has three erors.

Pranks for the memories, Jordan!!

Time flies like an arrow. Fruit flies like a banana.

# CRAZY Concoctions

## A Mad Scientist's Guide to Messy Mixtures

Jordan D. Brown
and
Dr. Viskus von Fickleschmutz

Illustrated by
Anthony Owsley

imagine!
Publishing

An Imagine Book
Published by Charlesbridge
85 Main Street, Watertown, MA 02472
(617) 926-0329
www.charlesbridge.com

The publisher does not have any control over and does not assume any responsibility
for author or third-party websites or their content.

Library of Congress Cataloging-in-Publication Data

Brown, Jordan.
Crazy concoctions : a mad scientist's guide to messy mixtures / by Jordan D. Brown.
    p. cm.
"An Imagine book."
ISBN 978-1-936140-51-0 (hardcover)
1. Science—Experiments—Juvenile literature. I. Title.
Q164.B86 2011
540.76—dc23
                    2011025660

2 4 6 8 10 9 7 5 3 1

For information about custom editions, special sales,
premium and corporate purchases, please contact
Charlesbridge Publishing at specialsales@charlesbridge.com

> To my wonderful wife, Ellen,
> with whom I've had great chemistry for more than twenty years.

## Acknowledgments

Many thanks to the creative team that collaborated on this book: Anthony Owsley, for his whimsical illustrations; Celia Naranjo, for designing the book with enthusiasm and attention to detail; and Kristin Ostby and Kate Ritchey, for their editorial expertise, patience, and smart suggestions. Chemistry consultants Nikae Perkinson and Stephen R. Duly, PhD, helped me understand the science behind the concoctions. Finally, thanks to Charles Nurnberg for inviting me to write another book for Charlesbridge Publishing. Here's to many more!

Special thanks to my delightful children, Finian and Olivia, for being a rich source of inspiration, laughter, and joy. I'm also grateful to Tanner for his tail wags, sweet licks, and long walks. My parents, Eileen and Stephen Brown, have always nurtured my creative efforts with boundless love and encouragement. Thanks to Allen Mogol, a great friend and talented writer, for his help, optimism, and clever ideas.

Finally, thanks to maverick scientist Dr. Viskus von Fickleschmutz for gracefully exiting when the publisher and I told him that his services were no longer needed.

OR NOT!!!
~F.

## READ THIS BEFORE YOU START
## YOUR FIRST EXPERIMENT!

I want you to have a terrific time as you explore your inner mad scientist. I want you to make marvelous messes, shout "Aww! Cool!" when you observe the chemical reactions, and even make your own discoveries. What I *don't* want is for anyone reading this book to get injured, damage household items, or get in trouble because they didn't read and respect the important safety rules on pages 10 and 11. So read those rules *first*! The publisher's pesky lawyers would like to point out that the author and the publisher are not responsible for the use or misuse of any experiment in this book. So play nicely, okay?

In this book, you'll find science experiments that are safe and fun for kids, but such activities can sometimes be unpredictable. That's why a smart young mad scientist should have a parent or other responsible grown-up around as he or she tries these concoctions. Besides, creating concoctions is a wonderful way for parents and kids to enjoy time together.

—Jordan D. Brown

# CONTENTS

# Are You a Mad Scientist?

Do you love making messy mixtures at home? Have you ever wondered why some combinations fizz and foam, while others magically morph into gooey glop? When you blend two totally random ingredients, do you laugh and get a crazy gleam in your eyes? If you answered *yes* to any of these questions, you just might be a mad scientist—like me!

I've enjoyed mucking around in the kitchen since I was a little boy. Long before I knew there were things called cookbooks with actual recipes, I had a blast inventing my own concoctions. My sister, Sharon, and I spent hours whipping up homemade mixtures of a hodgepodge of weird ingredients. Ketchup mixed with uncooked rice, salt, and chocolate sauce? Sure. Yogurt combined with shredded carrots, hot sauce, and green food coloring? Disgusting—but delightful! I nearly lost my mind the day I learned that putting together baking soda and vinegar causes a burst of bubbles. The possibilities were endless! Because of these joyful childhood experiments, I developed a lifelong passion for cooking and science.

THIS EXPERIMENT NEEDS AN ADULT MINION!

In this book, you'll discover some of my favorite formulas for making messy mixtures. You'll find a wacky liquid that changes color (page 50). You'll get a chance to whip up a gross mixture of bogus barf (page 24). There's even a chapter of amazing experiments you can eat (page 56)! Words in **bold** throughout the book are defined in the Glossary (page 77). Before you start, make sure to read the important safety rules (page 10) to keep you and everything around you safe while you're experimenting. When you see the icon on the left, be sure to have a grown-up by your side as you concoct your creations.

In addition to giving you step-by-step directions, I've included explanations of the chemistry behind the mixtures. **Chemistry** is the science of what stuff is made of, and how different chemicals react together. Some of these ideas can be tricky to understand, but if you have some idea about why the concoctions work, you'll be better prepared to invent your own marvelous mixtures.

## Happy experimenting!

Jordan D. Brown

P.S. A special shout-out to Dr. Viskus von Fickleschmutz, the guy who was originally hired to cowrite this book:

Hey, Dr. F, sorry things didn't work out with our collaboration. No hard feelings. It was a blast meeting a truly *mad* mad scientist and visiting your lab. Your silly pranks were fun, but the experiments you suggested were *way* too dangerous for a kids' book. (Mind-altering potions? Exploding chickens? What were you thinking?!) Anyway, I hope you are finally getting the help you need. I hear great things about the Hansburg Hospital for the Diabolically Angry. Thanks, by the way, for your recent e-mail congratulating me on finishing this book. But what did you mean by "It ain't over 'til it's over?"—JDB

Hey, Jordan,
I'm sorry I wasn't able to cowrite this book with you. What's the big idea of getting me kicked off the project??? After all the laughs and banana-sardine smoothies we shared, I would have thought you'd be grateful! Cmon, I told you your hair would grow back! Geez, some people can't take a joke. You were asleep, and I had a batch of my balding concoction. What's a mad scientist supposed to do? Well, don't worry. I used my superior intelligence to get my hands on your book just before it was printed. I've added my expertise for your lucky readers. Oh, and nice mustache, dude!

-Dr. Fickleschmutz

# IMPORTANT SAFETY RULES & TIPS
## Read This Before You Start!

Being a mad scientist at home can be loads of fun, but don't be foolish. Danger is one ingredient you definitely *don't* want to mix into your concoctions! Anytime you perform chemistry experiments, the most important rule is BE SAFE. If you follow these safety rules, you will avoid getting yourself or a friend sick or injured, and you won't have an adult shouting things like, "Who used up all the vegetable oil?" or "Why is there green goo all over the dog?!"

- **Dress for a mess.** Pull back any long hair, take off any jewelry that could hang down into your ingredients, and wear old clothes that you don't mind getting dirty or permanently stained.

- **Wash your hands.** Before and after you do each experiment, wash your hands with soap and warm water for at least twenty seconds (as long as it takes you to sing "Happy Birthday" twice).

- **Read all the directions before you start mixing.** Be prepared. Don't just look at the pictures, say, "Oh, I know what to do!" and zoom ahead. Otherwise, the experiments might not work out. Also, by reading all the directions first, you can make sure you have all the necessary ingredients for that particular experiment before you get started. (All the materials in these experiments are inexpensive and can be easily found in supermarkets, drug stores, hardware stores, or craft shops.)

- **Don't fool with the formulas.** Mixing household ingredients together can be safe, but some combinations can be very dangerous. So make sure to stick to the safe formulas in this book. (At the end of the book, I'll give you some guidelines for inventing your own concoctions!)

- **Keep your concoctions away from your eyes, ears, nose, and mouth.** Keep all your homemade mixtures away from any place where they could enter your body unless the directions say it's okay.

Jordan, how come YOU didn't wash your hands after you used the bathroom in my lab? Didn't think I saw you, huh?

- **Wear goggles and rubber gloves.** If the directions say to wear rubber gloves or safety goggles, please do so. A messy mixture on your skin or in your eyes could be harmful to you.

- **Ask an adult's permission before you use a bunch of any one ingredient.** For some experiments, you might need a lot of one ingredient, such as vegetable oil or cornstarch. Just make sure that it's okay before you start experimenting.

- **Wash your materials between experiments.** Make a point of cleaning all bowls, spoons, and cups after you complete an experiment. That way you won't accidentally combine ingredients that don't belong together. When doing a messy experiment, you might want to use plastic cups or spoons that can be thrown away when you're done.

- **Have paper towels and sponges handy.** You never know when a spill or mess will happen.

- ***Never* eat your concoctions unless the experiment explicitly states it's okay.** Some of the materials in these experiments could make you very sick if you swallowed them. Likewise, be careful not to leave out any of your concoctions where someone (your sister, the dog, a neighbor) might drink them. The exception to this rule is Chapter 5, which features recipes for mixtures that were designed to be tasted.

- **Pick your "lab" carefully.** Chemistry experiments can get messy, so don't create a concoction on your grandma's antique sofa or another difficult-to-clean area. Even on a "safe" surface, such as a kitchen table, you might want to put down a plastic bag or newspaper to protect the surface. And if you spill anything, clean it up right away. If the weather is good, many of these experiments can be done outside, too. If you're not sure of the best place to set up your lab or how to protect the area, ask an adult.

- **Put grown-ups to work.** Anytime you see the icon on the right, ask a grown-up to help you. This is especially important if the experiment involves using anything that could be dangerous, such as a sharp knife or a microwave oven.

THIS EXPERIMENT NEEDS AN ADULT MINION!

- **Don't throw goo or slime down the drain (or down the toilet).** When you're done playing with any slimy or gloppy concoctions you create, wrap them in a plastic garbage bag and toss them in the trash. Otherwise, you could seriously mess up the pipes in your house. The plumber might love you for giving him business, but your parents won't be pleased.

Jordan, my man, you forgot to tell your readers these VERY IMPORTANT experimenting tips!
- Crack a raw egg in your underpants! (So cool, so slippery!)
- Whenever you read the word "chemical" in this book, drink a glass of prune juice.
- If at first you don't succeed, don't skydive.
- If you ever meet a girl named Molly Cule, make fun of her name.
- Feeling depressed? Three words: slime hand puppets!

# CHAPTER 1

# Slime and Goo

Yay, it's slime time! One of life's big joys is whipping up a bowl of goo—and then squishing your hands in it. It's easy to make a wild mad scientist laugh when your fingers are dripping with colorful ooze! In this chapter, you'll experiment with different kinds of goo and slime, and uncover their slippery secrets.

You mean the classic "Bwaaaahahahahahahahaha!!" Or the lesser known but just as effective "Hoooba Dooba Nooba!!!"

—F.

# Gooey Glop

This strange stuff can either flow like a liquid or be rolled up into a ball like a solid. It all depends on how much pressure you put on it.

## Stuff You Need

- 2 cups cornstarch
- 2 cups water
- food coloring
- measuring cups
- large bowl
- small bowl
- metal spoon
- ziplock bag (for storage)

## Steps

1. Pour 2 cups of cornstarch into a large bowl. Pick up some cornstarch and rub it between your fingers. Cornstarch feels kind of like flour, right? Cooks use cornstarch to thicken gravy and sauces. Mad scientists mix it with water to explore its weird changing consistency.

   *I always rub some on my elbows for good luck... but only if it's a Wednesday in October!*

2. In a small bowl, pour 2 cups of water. Then drip in 3 to 5 drops of food coloring. Stir with a spoon until it's blended and you like the color. (You can do this experiment without the food coloring, but your glop will be white.) Try not to get any food coloring on your hands or clothes, as it will stain them.

   **TIP:** If you do get food coloring on your skin, it's no big deal. You can wash it with soap and water, then rub it with a small amount of shaving cream or toothpaste. If the stain remains, soak a paper towel in vinegar, then rub it on the stained parts of your hand. Then wash your hands with soap and water again.

   *And, BOOM, your hands will then STINK from vinegar! Yuckarooni!*

3. Time to create the glop! Add the colored water to the cornstarch a little at a time. You'll see that the water and cornstarch won't combine at first. That's why you need to stick your hands into the mixture and squish together the ingredients. Keep mixing with your hands until you can't see any of the cornstarch powder. To get just the right consistency, you might need to add more cornstarch or more water.

4. Play with your gooey glop!

   - Slowly press your fingers into the glop.
   - Quickly poke the surface of the glop with a finger, or slap it with the palm of your hand.
   - Grab a small amount of the glop in your hands and see if you can roll it into a ball. How long does the ball hold its shape?
   - Stick a metal spoon into the bowl and slowly stir it around. Now try stirring the mixture quickly. What happens?
   - Offer to shampoo your mom's hair with gooey glop!

5. You can store your gooey glop or toss it. To store it, put it in the refrigerator in a sealable plastic container or ziplock bag. Don't leave it in there too long, or mold could grow on it. If you decide to throw it away, do *not* put it down the sink right away. First, add lots (at least 3–4 cups) of water to the cornstarch mixture so it turns into a thin liquid. Then you can safely pour it down the drain or flush it in the toilet.

*If you ever visit my hometown of Bnozgzerkurplanzd, be sure to visit the Mold Zoo.*

## Hmmm... What's Going On?

A famous scientist in the 1600s, **Sir Isaac Newton**, believed that all liquids keep the same viscosity no matter how much pressure you put on them. **Viscosity** is the fancy science word for how easily a liquid flows—or doesn't. For example, honey has a greater viscosity than water does because it pours more slowly. Liquids like these move or flow the same way, regardless of the force you put on them. It doesn't matter whether you stir them fast or slow—the spoon always moves through the liquid with the same resistance, or push-back.

Not so with gooey glop! When you stir it slowly, the spoon gently glides through the liquid. But when you stir it quickly, the material pushes back on the spoon, making it very hard to stir. As you discovered, you can even yank out a "ball" of gooey glop and roll it around in your hands. Once you stop putting pressure on the ball, though, it becomes ooze again. The more force you put on the glop (by rolling, poking, or stirring it), the more it acts like a solid.

Scientists called stuff like gooey glop non-Newtonian fluids, because they break Newton's rules about how liquids should behave. Silly Putty is another example of a non-Newtonian fluid. When you slowly stretch it, it oozes into a thin string; but when you quickly pull a blob of Silly Putty in two different directions, it breaks into two pieces with flat edges. Quicksand is also a non-Newtonian fluid. If you struggle to escape from it, you actually make it harder for yourself to move!

Isaac, how do your three laws apply to an apple pie in your face??? ~F.

**Sir Isaac Newton**

# Oops! ACCIDENTS IN CHEMISTRY

## THE INVENTION OF SILLY PUTTY

During World War II in the 1940s, the U.S. government needed lots of rubber to make truck tires, soldiers' boots, and more. Rubber is made from a white liquid called latex that some trees and plants give off instead of sap. Most of the world's latex comes from the inner bark of the hevea, or rubber tree, in Brazil. Getting all that latex was very expensive, so scientists tried to figure out a way to make fake rubber.

One day in 1943, a scientist named James Wright dropped boric acid into silicone oil and discovered a bouncy, stretchy goo. It could stand up to both extreme heat and extreme cold. The company that Wright worked for, General Electric (GE), told all their scientists about this material, which it nicknamed Nutty Putty. No one was very impressed. Then, in 1949, an unemployed man named Peter Hodgson saw some of this putty at a party. He thought it might be a great toy for kids, so he bought a bunch of it from GE and hired someone to break it into one-ounce pieces. He renamed it Silly Putty and packaged it in plastic eggs, because it was almost Easter.

After several years of struggling, it became an international hit! In fact, in 1968, the Apollo 8 astronauts used it to hold down some of their tools once they left Earth's gravity.

# Talk Like a Scientist

*blah, blah, blah...*

# STATES OF MATTER

Everything in the world—from oceans to computers to zucchini to YOU—is made of stuff called matter. **Matter** is anything that takes up space. On our planet, matter is found primarily in three different categories: solid, liquid, and gas.

Each kind of matter is made of itty-bitty bits of stuff called **molecules**. In a solid, such as the pages in this book, the molecules are packed very closely together and don't move much. In a liquid, like a glass of lemonade, the molecules move around more quickly, which is why you can pour a liquid, but can't pour a solid. In a gas, like the air around us, the molecules are spread out and move very quickly, so they can float away if they're not contained.

It is possible for the same kind of material to change from a solid to a liquid to a gas. Take an ice cube: It starts out as a solid, but if you let it melt, it becomes a liquid (water). And if you boil that water, it becomes a gas (steam). Even though solids, liquids, and gases are the most typical kinds of matter on Earth, the most common state of matter in the universe is plasma. Plasma is a supercharged gas. Stars like our sun, as well as lightning, are made of plasma.

I recently invented a new state of matter called "watsa"...as in "Watsa matter with you?"

## Silly Science Online

## A Pool of Goop

Slapping your hand on a bowl full of cornstarch and water is messy fun, but could you run barefoot across a big pool of the stuff? That's the question some curious scientists with a lot of time (and cornstarch) on their hands wanted to find out. After using a cement mixer to combine thousands of pounds of cornstarch mixed with water in a large pool, some mad scientists took off their shoes and ran across it. Guess what? Because gooey glop is a non-Newtonian fluid, they didn't sink! Want to see it for yourself? Go online and search for "water and cornstarch pool video" and you'll be treated to several versions of this crazy experiment.

## It's Alive!!

Some other mad scientists wanted to make their cornstarch-and-water mixtures look alive, so they placed some gooey glop on a stereo speaker. Then they blasted repetitive low-pitched sounds through the speaker. The vibrations caused the glop to wiggle in really interesting ways! If you want to see this for yourself, do an Internet search for "cornstarch monster video." You'll see cornstarch do the boogie like it never has before.

Never, NEVER go skinny-dipping in a gooey glop pool! Because you could get arrested and an embarrassing photo could end up on the front page of Mad Scientist Daily. Or so I've heard...

# Be the Wizard of Ooze

Mix together a few ingredients, and a colorful blob of squishy, slimy wonderfulness will appear before your eyes!

## Stuff You Need

- 1 8-ounce bottle of white glue (such as Elmer's)
- 1½ cups warm water
- food coloring
- ¼ cup glow-in-the-dark paint (optional) (available at craft stores)
- 1 teaspoon of Borax powder (found in the laundry aisle of the supermarket)
- measuring spoons
- measuring cups
- medium bowl that you can throw away
- large plastic cup that you can throw away
- plastic spoons
- ziplock bag (for storage)

**SAFETY NOTE:** Borax is safe when used in small amounts. But in large doses it can be dangerous, so make sure to keep the box and this slime away from children younger than age five and any pets. Clean up any powder spills right away. And *don't* eat it!

## Steps

1. Squeeze a whole bottle of white glue into a medium bowl that you can throw away.

2. Refill the empty glue bottle to the top with warm water, screw the lid on, and shake it. Then empty the water into the same bowl as the glue. Put a few drops of food coloring into this water-glue mixture, until you like the color, and stir with a plastic spoon. (Be careful not to get food coloring on your hands or clothes because it will stain. See page 13 for tips on removing food coloring from your skin.)

**Optional step:** If you want to make your goo glow, mix in ¼ cup of glow-in-the-dark paint instead of food coloring. Once your ooze is finished, hold it near a bright lightbulb—but not too close! Then turn off the lights and watch it glow!

I'll bet you can't say "goo glow" three times fast!

18

3. Fill a plastic cup with ½ cup of warm water, add 1 teaspoon of Borax, and stir with a different plastic spoon. It's okay if all the powder doesn't dissolve.

4. Slowly pour the Borax solution into the water-glue mixture. Now the fun part! Squish it all together with your hands. Chemical bonds will form, and you'll have a fresh batch of awesome ooze! Lift it up and admire it. (Don't worry if there's some extra water left in the bowl. You can toss it.)

5. Play with your ooze! Stretch it slowly, let it drip from your fingers, and make your own gooey discoveries.

6. When you're done, store the ooze in a ziplock bag to keep it from drying out.

*Trying to conquer the world can be VERY frustrating. To cheer myself up, I rub this ooze in my armpits. Ahh... it's as slippery as a slimy eel!*

## Hmmm... What's Going On?

Scientists call the ooze you just made a polymer. **Polymers** are materials that are made of long chains of the same kind of molecule. Molecules are so super-small, we can't see them. But if just one molecule were the size of a paper clip, then a polymer might be as long as a swimming pool. Plastic bags, Silly Putty, Jell-O, rubber bands, plastic toys, and chewing gum are example of polymers. Naturally occurring polymers include hair, nails, cotton, and DNA.

To help you think about polymers, imagine you had a bunch of rubber bands. These bands would act in different ways depending on how they were attached together. If you looped them into a long chain, they would be much stronger and more flexible than just one rubber band. If you wound them around one another to make a rubber band ball, it would be hard, but bouncy.

# THE INVENTION OF CELLULOID

*You old grouch! Maybe a cheap plastic beanie will make you smile!*

~F.

**John Wesley Hyatt**

Today, plastics are everywhere. Toothbrushes, computers, and many toys are made of this stuff. The reason plastics are so popular is that they are lightweight, inexpensive, sturdy, and, when heated up, can be molded into any shape.

But two hundred years ago, nothing was made of plastic. Why? Because no one had invented it yet. One of the first plastics was invented in the 1860s.

**John Wesley Hyatt**, a printer from New York, heard about a contest offered by a big billiards company. Billiards is the name for the hard balls that are knocked around on a pool table with pool cues. At that time, playing billiards was wildly popular. The problem was that billiards were made from ivory, which comes from elephant tusks. Thousands of elephants had to be killed in order to get this material. So the billiards company offered a $10,000 prize to anyone who could come up with another material for creating billiards.

During his many experiments, Hyatt found success when he mixed together guncotton (a black powder used in explosives) with camphor and alcohol in a pressure-cooking machine. He created a gooey material that could be easily molded but got very hard when it cooled down. He didn't win the contest because of one small problem: When billiards made of this material smashed into one another, they burst into flames! Eventually, in 1870, Hyatt and his brother Isaiah reworked this material into something they called celluloid. This material was used to make buttons, false teeth, camera film, and much more. Today, celluloid is still used to make Ping-Pong balls, eyeglass frames, and the covering for piano keys.

# Sculpting Slime

The only problem with slime and goo is that they won't stay put. The great thing about the stuff in this experiment is that you can use it to create works of art that last a long time! They also make groovy gifts.

## Stuff You Need

- 2 teaspoons of Borax powder (found in the laundry aisle of the supermarket)
- ¾ cup warm water
- ¼ cup white glue (such as Elmer's)
- food coloring
- 1 cup polystyrene beads (available at craft stores as bean bag or doll filler)
  **NOTE:** You can also break up a Styrofoam cup or a Styrofoam egg carton into tiny pieces to substitute for the beads.
- measuring spoons
- measuring cups
- 2 large plastic cups
- ziplock bag

## Steps

1. In a large plastic cup, mix 2 teaspoons of Borax into ½ cup of warm water and stir until the powder is dissolved.

2. In a second cup, mix ¼ cup of white glue and ¼ cup of warm water. Stir a few drops of food coloring into the glue-water mixture.

3. Pour the glue mixture and 1 cup of polystyrene beads into a ziplock bag. Carefully pour in the Borax solution. Squeeze out the extra air, and zip the bag closed. Knead it with your hands until it is well combined.

Ooh! Two pony tails!

Make your very own Dr. Fickleschmutz action figure! This is what I look like!

What a HANDSOME devil! ~F.

4. Remove the slime from the bag and mold it into an interesting shape. You can braid it, build a slime snowman, invent your own type of animal, and much more. Let your imagination run wild!

5. Let your molded slime dry. It will hold its shape forever. Store any leftover sculpting slime in a sealed bag in the refrigerator (unless you want it covered in fuzzy mold... yuck).

Last week, I discovered that my girlfriend Olga's feet were covered in a funky fungus. Yuckarooni!!

## Hmmm... What's Going On?

How do the polystyrene beads let you mold the goo into different shapes? They give the goo something solid to form around so that it doesn't wiggle as much. Think of those tasty dessert bars made with crispy rice cereal and melted marshmallows. When the marshmallows are heated up, they form a sticky liquid that doesn't hold a shape. When you mix the dry crispy rice cereal into the sticky marshmallow mixture, though, the concoction you end up with is moldable. In the case of sculpting slime, the beads are like crispy rice, since they give the slime a sturdier structure. But don't eat the sculpting slime!

**FUN FACT**

Styrofoam is about 98% air.

Jordan, I've heard the same thing about your head!

# CHAPTER 2

# Totally Gross

The disgusting mixtures in this chapter will help you create yucky stuff that looks amazingly like vomit, blood, and boogers. With a little practice, you'll get these concoctions to look like they came out of your body rather than out of your kitchen. So put on some old clothes, grab your supplies, and let's get mixing!

Jordan,

I've got a yuckety yuck-yuck for ya: What's the difference between boogers and broccoli?

Kids don't eat broccoli!

-F.

# Pretend Puke

Phony vomit from a toy store is nice, but it can't beat vomit actually made out of food! The stuff you're about to make looks gross—but it smells fine, so you *probably* won't throw up... The secret to creating good fake vomit (now *there's* a sentence you don't see too often) is to combine a bunch of ingredients that look like partly digested food, then hold them together with a jiggly goo made from gelatin!

## Stuff You Need

- 3 tablespoons water
- ⅓ cup applesauce
- ½ teaspoon instant coffee OR cocoa powder
- 1 package of unflavored gelatin
- 1 tablespoon oatmeal OR 1 tablespoon of cornflakes, roughly crushed
- 1 tablespoon corn (optional)
- 1 tablespoon carrot bits (optional)
- measuring spoons
- measuring cups
- bowl
- spoon
- rubber spatula
- microwave-safe plate
- parchment paper
- microwave oven
- *$1 million, to send to me, Dr. Fickleschmutz*

## Steps

1. First, pour 3 tablespoons of water into a bowl. Add ⅓ cup of applesauce and stir.

2. With a grown-up's help, microwave the applesauce mixture until it is very hot (about 1–2 minutes). Have the grown-up carefully remove it from the microwave.

3. Stir in ½ teaspoon of instant coffee (or cocoa powder) and the whole package of unflavored gelatin.

4. Mix in 1 tablespoon of oatmeal (or crushed corn flakes). Mix until well blended. At this point, you can add a tablespoon of corn or carrot bits for extra color.

5. Use a spoon to drop some of this bogus barf mixture onto a microwave-safe plate that's been covered with parchment paper. You're going for the splatter factor here, so drop it from a foot above the paper. You can also use a rubber spatula to spread out the mixture.

6. Refrigerate the plate for 3–4 hours, until the mixture has a hardened, rubbery texture.

*This would be a good time to do the hokey-pokey and turn yourself around.*

7. Use a rubber spatula to gently remove the bogus barf and place it on a table, a tiled or wood floor, or another hard surface. (You don't want to get it stuck all over the carpet!)

8. Plan a good prank to fool someone. For instance, when someone comes into the room where your bogus barf is sitting, announce, "Look what I found! Someone puked!"

*-Hurled!*
*-Ralphed!*
*-Wretched!*
*-Blew chunks!*
*-Heaved!*
*-Upchucked!*
*-Tossed their cookies!*
*-Lost their lunch!*
*-Made a gastric geyser!*

*I'm crazy for gross expressions. What are YOUR favorites?*

## Hmmm... What's Going On?

Gelatin, the active ingredient in Jell-O, is a polymer. The collagen used to make gelatin comes from pig and cow skin and bones! After these animal products are ground up, they are treated to release the collagen. It is boiled, and the top layer of gelatin is removed for use. The molecules are in long, jiggly chains, and when they are in cold water, the proteins that make them up stick together.

Why didn't the fake puke stick to the parchment paper? That's because this special paper is coated with a layer of silicone. Silicone is a polymer that pushes away water and grease. It has a very high melting temperature (2,577°F), so even in a hot oven, it won't melt. Many bakers use parchment paper when making cookies.

## Talk Like a Scientist

*OK, Dmitri, if you're so smart, you tell me what the basic elements of spray-on cheese are! ~F.*

# Elements and Atoms

Everything in the universe—from planets to petunias to pickles—is made up of different chemicals. And all these chemicals are made up of the same "building blocks" called elements. **Elements** are chemicals that are made of only one type of atom. **Atoms** are the tiniest pieces of an element. Think of atoms as letters of the alphabet. You can put letters together in different ways to make words, just like atoms make up elements. And words can be arranged into sentences, like different elements can be formed into chemicals. Gold, oxygen, neon, and aluminum are some elements you probably know already. There are also some other elements with weird names, such as californium, strontium, rubidium, and einsteinium. (That last one is, of course, named after the famous scientist Albert Einstein.)

There are 118 known elements. Ninety-nine percent of your body is made up of only six elements: hydrogen, oxygen, carbon, nitrogen, calcium, and phosphorus.

All the elements are organized in a famous chart called the periodic table, created by the Russian scientist **Dmitri Mendeleev** in 1869. On the chart, elements that have similar features are grouped together. All the light gases, like hydrogen and helium, are together, as are all the metals, such as gold and silver.

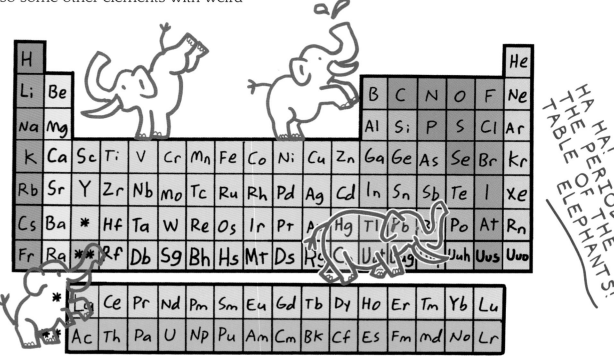

HA HA! THE PERIODIC TABLE OF THE ELEPHANTS!

# Bogus Boogers

THIS EXPERIMENT NEEDS AN ADULT MINION!

*A-a-a-choo!!!* **Making fake snot is a great way to explore the science of polymers—or simply to gross out your family.**

*Why didn't you let me include my recipe for exploding boogers?? All you need is a few drops of lotasnotium, a smidge of gelatin, and a dash of honey. One pretend sneeze from that concoction—and* **ka-BOOM!**

## Stuff You Need

- ½ cup water
- 3 packages of unflavored gelatin
- green and yellow food coloring
- ¼ cup light corn syrup
- measuring cups
- microwave-safe bowl OR saucepan
- microwave oven OR stove
- oven mitts
- spoon
- another bowl
- fork
- ziplock bag (for storage)

## Steps

1. Pour ½ cup of water into a microwave-safe bowl. Heat it for about 2–3 minutes, just until the water boils.

   **NOTE:** If you don't have a microwave oven, you can heat up this concoction in a saucepan on the stove. Either way, make sure you have a grown-up handy.

2. Using oven mitts, put the bowl on a heat-safe surface. Empty 3 packages of unflavored gelatin into the water and stir. Add a few drops of green and yellow food coloring to give it a lovely snotty appearance.

GESUNDHEIT!

3. Let it stand for 1–2 minutes, then pour it into a separate bowl.

4. Pour in about ¼ cup of light corn syrup and stir.

5. Once the mixture has cooled to room temperature, use a fork to pick up the strands of homemade snot. If it's too thick, stir in some extra warm water. Once you have the right consistency, you can touch it with your fingers.

6. Use it! For a prank, you could walk near a table when someone's eating and say, "Excuse me, I've got to sneeze." Turn your head away from the table and say, "Ah… Ah… Ah… (pause) Naw, it went away!" Then, a few minutes later, repeat this almost-sneeze, and have the sneeze urge stop. Say something like, "I'd better get a tissue; I feel like there's this big sneeze that wants to get out." Return with a handful of fake snot secretly covered with a tissue. Repeat the almost-sneeze act yet again… but this time, let out a huge *ACHOOOO!* Let the tissue fall and the fake boogers fly.

7. Store your snot in a ziplock bag when you're not using it. Toss it in the trash when you're done.

# COOL FACTS… Real-Life Snot

How are real boogers made? The nose knows. And now you will, too!

Scientists call the little blobs of goo that live in your nose mucus. Your own personal snot factory (in your nose and the surrounding air-filled spaces called sinuses) cranks out about a quart of snot every day. *Yeeech!* Mucus is not just there to be gross, though. It protects the inside of your body, especially your lungs. In addition to oxygen, which your body needs, the air you breathe is filled with stuff your body doesn't need, like dust, dirt, and germs. That's why mucus is sticky. It traps that stuff in your nose, far away from your lungs.

*Says who?!*

When all the trapped stuff gets caught in the mucus, it forms clumps known as boogers. Picking your nose might seem like a smart way to clear it out, but boogers are loaded with germs. A smarter idea is to blast all that gunk into a tissue and throw it away.

# Fake Blood

THIS EXPERIMENT NEEDS AN ADULT MINION!

Using ketchup for pretend blood is for amateurs! Here's the messy mixture you need to make if you want to fool others into thinking your pretend bloody boo-boos are real. Start with a make-believe paper cut, then move on to a full-blown hemorrhage. But make sure you reveal the truth quickly—or you might have an unconscious family member on your hands!

## FUN FACT
In the old days, when movies were only made in black-and-white, the special effects artists sometimes used chocolate syrup for pretend blood.

## Stuff You Need

- 1 cup red fruit punch
- 2 tablespoons cornstarch
- 1 cup light corn syrup
- 2 tablespoons red food coloring
- 2 tablespoons chocolate syrup OR cocoa powder
- few drops green or blue food coloring
- plastic, newspapers, or other surface covering
- measuring spoons
- measuring cups
- blender or glass container with tight-fitting lid
- paper towels
- ziplock bag (for storage)

AAAAAAAAARRGH!

Food coloring also stains bunnies!

## Steps

1. Cover your work area with plastic, newspapers, or another protective covering. This is not a good experiment to do near carpets, wooden tables, or other surfaces that could be permanently stained. Food coloring can stain countertops, clothes, and skin.

   **TIP:** If you do get some on a counter, a grown-up can use a sponge and some bleach powder to clean it off. See page 13 for tips on removing food coloring stains from your skin.

2. Have a grown-up help you mix together 1 cup of fruit punch and 2 tablespoons of cornstarch in a blender. (If you don't have a blender, you can put the ingredients in a plastic container with a tight-fitting lid and shake it up.)

3. Pour in 1 cup of light corn syrup, 2 tablespoons of red food coloring, and 2 tablespoons of chocolate syrup (or cocoa powder), and blend. Does it look like blood yet? If not, add a few drops of green or blue food coloring, and blend again.

4. Now it's time for a test. Bunch up a paper towel, dip it into your fake blood, and rub a small amount of it on your finger or arm. Look realistic? If not, add some more red, green, or blue food coloring (just a drop at a time) until the color looks just right. You can store your fake blood in a ziplock bag in the fridge.

5. Plan a good prank to fool someone. Maybe try out a nosebleed: Put on some old clothes you don't mind getting stained. Then put 1 tablespoon of fake blood inside a small ziplock bag, squeezing out the extra air before you seal it. Cut a tiny hole in one corner of the bag. Next, wrap a few paper towels around it. Say to your victim, "I think I'm getting a nosebleed! Ahhh!" Then hold the paper towels near your nose as you gently squeeze the bag, letting it squirt on the paper towels and your hands. (Be careful not to get the fake blood on anything but the paper towels and your hands!)

And don't spray the fake blood all over Jordan's computer. Surprisingly, he doesn't like it.

Bags of blood love being near the packages of raw hamburger meat. It's like a homecoming!

## COOL FACTS...
### Real-Life Blood

Everyone agrees that blood that squirts out of our bodies is red. But some people think that blood inside our bodies is blue, and then turns red when it hits the air. They say that the oxygen in the air is what changes the blood's color. Not true! This myth probably got started when people noticed the bluish veins near the surface of their skin and thought, "The blood inside the veins must be blue!" But actually, the blue color you see is just a trick of the light on your skin. The blood in your veins is as red as the blood anywhere else in your body.

# CHAPTER 3

# That's Gas-tastic!

Now it's time to get things fizzing, foaming, and bubbling. In this chapter, you'll find out some wonderful ways to get some great reactions—both from the chemicals you're mixing and from the faces of your friends and family! You'll also learn the science behind Pop Rocks candy, and get to explore how gas can be a very strong force.

I just released some very stinky gas. Lucky for you, this book isn't the scratch-n-sniff kind...
—F.

# Big... Bigger... *BOOM!*

**THIS EXPERIMENT NEEDS AN ADULT MINION!**

Ziplock bags are pretty strong—unless you fill them with two chemicals that produce lots of gas. So mix, shake, and stand back!

*Awww, you're no fun, Jordan!*

**WARNING:** This experiment could have EXPLOSIVE results. Nothing dangerous, of course. But just to be on the safe side, protect your eyes with goggles, dress in old clothes, and make sure to have a goggle-and-old-clothes-wearing grown-up there to help you. *And don't do this experiment with a live cobra nearby, because it might bite you. See? I'm concerned about safety, too!*

## Stuff You Need

- 1 tablespoon baking soda
- ¾ cup white vinegar
- ¼ cup warm water
- plastic, newspapers, or other surface covering
- safety goggles
- quart-size ziplock bags
- paper towels
- measuring spoons
- measuring cup
- small plastic funnel
- *something that rhymes with "kreltopnifcus"*

*beach towels as big as a football field*

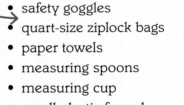

## Steps

1. Cover your work area with plastic, newspapers, or other protective covering, or try this experiment in a place you can get wet and messy, like a bathtub or outside. Put on goggles to protect your eyes.

2. Test a quart-size ziplock bag to make sure it doesn't have any holes. Fill it with water to check for leaks. Then empty out the water.

3. Cut a square piece of paper towel about 6" by 6". Put 1 tablespoon of baking soda in the middle of the paper towel, and fold the towel in both directions so that the baking soda is trapped in a little packet. Don't tape the packet closed because you'll want it to release the baking soda later in this activity.

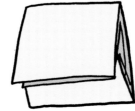

4. Using a small plastic funnel, pour ¾ cup of white vinegar and ¼ cup of warm water into the ziplock bag. Seal the bag and shake it.

5. Open the bag halfway. Insert the baking soda packet in the top of the bag and pinch it there to hold it away from the liquid. Seal the bag *tightly*! Double-check to make sure it is totally closed.

6. Let the baking soda packet drop into the vinegar mixture. Shake the bag so the baking soda and liquid mix, then quickly set it down and step back. What happens? What do you think is going on?

7. Get a new ziplock bag, or clean and dry the old one. Repeat the experiment with different amounts of vinegar and baking soda. Make predictions before you do any mixing. Ask yourself things like, "What will happen if I put double the amount of baking soda, but keep the amount of vinegar the same?" Or "What would happen if I doubled *both* ingredients? Or tripled them?" (You might find it useful to use a bigger ziplock bag for the larger quantities of baking soda and vinegar.) You could also try this experiment using cold water, or no water at all, to see how it affects the results.

## Hmmm... What's Going On?

Why does mixing baking soda and vinegar make so many bubbles? When baking soda (known to chemists as sodium bicarbonate) and vinegar (a weak acid) get together, they go through a chemical change. A **chemical change** happens when two or more chemicals rearrange and change into a different chemical or chemicals. The chemicals that make up baking soda and those in vinegar trade their tiny parts and create new substances: a liquid (water), a solid dissolved in the water (sodium acetate), and a gas (carbon dioxide).

As you probably know, carbon dioxide is one of the gases you breathe out—and plants "breathe" in. All explosions are chemical reactions that produce a lot of gas very rapidly.

# COOL FACTS... Baking Soda

- Baking soda powder starts out as a natural mineral in the ground called trona. Most of the trona in the United States comes from Wyoming.

- Scientists call baking soda by its official name, sodium bicarbonate. It has the chemical formula $NaHCO_3$.

- The first bubbly soda ever sold was lemonade mixed with a small amount of baking soda. The baking soda mixed with the citric acid in the lemon juice made the bubbles (carbon dioxide).

- When food starts to go bad in your refrigerator, it often produces acids. Putting an open box of baking soda in your fridge can make it a less stinky place by absorbing these kinds of odors.

- In 1986, for the Statue of Liberty's one hundredth anniversary celebration, more than 100 tons of baking soda were used to clean the statue's interior copper walls.

# Pop Rocks Power

For many years, there has been a rumor that a kid ate a whole package of Pop Rocks candy then drank a can of soda, and his stomach exploded! You'll be relieved to know this could never happen. Yes, this concoction does produce carbon dioxide, but only a small amount. (You probably *would* get a big bellyache from downing all that sugar, though!) In this experiment, you can use the power of Pop Rocks to blow up a small balloon.

*My crazy cousin Unkchewus once ate a bucket of Pop Rocks, then guzzled ten gallons of soda! He was burping for weeks!*

## Stuff You Need

- 1–2 packages of Pop Rocks candy
- water
- 1 16-ounce bottle of soda
- 1 cup vinegar
- 1 tablespoon baking soda
- plate
- metal spoon
- small funnel
- 2 small balloons
- measuring spoons
- measuring cups
- a fuchsia baseball hat

POP! crackle! POP! pop! crackle!

## Steps

1. Sprinkle a few Pop Rocks in your mouth. What do you think causes that crazy crackling sound?

2. How else can you get the Pop Rocks to make that popping sound? Pour some Pop Rocks on a plate. What happens if you pour water on them? What if you squish them with the back of a metal spoon?

3. Time to use the power of Pop Rocks and soda to inflate a balloon! Use a plastic funnel to pour a package of Pop Rocks into an uninflated balloon.

4. Take off the top of a 16-ounce bottle of soda. Without allowing the Pop Rocks to fall into the soda bottle, stretch the neck of the balloon around the bottle's rim.

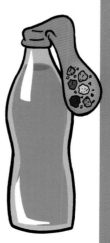

# The Story Behind...
# POP ROCKS

In the 1950s, chemist **William A. Mitchell** was trying to figure out a formula for making "instant soda." The idea was, rather than buying liquid soda in a bottle, you could sprinkle a powder into some plain water and it would transform into a bubbly, sugary drink. Mitchell figured out a way to cram lots of bubbles into hard candy powder, but the "instant soda" idea never took off. Twenty years later, another chemist at the General Foods company found Mitchell's formula, revised it a bit, and Pop Rocks were born!

**William A. Mitchell**

*Only you, my friend, have ever come close to matching my true genius! Pop Rocks rule!*

5. When you're ready, lift the balloon upright to release the Pop Rocks into the soda bottle. Watch what happens!

6. Try a variation of this experiment for comparison: Empty out and clean the soda bottle you used for the Pop Rocks experiment. Fill it with 1 cup of vinegar. Then use the plastic funnel to fill a new balloon with about 1 tablespoon of baking soda. When you're ready, lift the balloon to drop the baking soda into the bottle. Watch what happens. Which produces more bubbles, the Pop Rocks and soda concoction, or the baking soda and vinegar one?

## Hmmm... What's Going On?

What are Pop Rocks made of? Why do they crackle when you wet or crush them? Pop Rocks are made of the same basic ingredients that lollipops are made of: sugar, corn syrup, water, and flavoring. What makes Pop Rocks different is that, when the candy is still a liquid in the factory, it is pumped with *lots* of carbon dioxide gas (600 pounds per square inch). When the candy hardens, these tiny gas bubbles get trapped. When the candy melts in your mouth or is crushed, the bubbles pop as the gas is released.

Why did the balloon blow up? The bottle was filled with soda (or vinegar) and air at the start. When you mixed the chemicals (either Pop Rocks and soda, or baking soda and vinegar), this created more carbon dioxide in the closed space. The extra gas had to go somewhere, so it escaped into the flexible balloon. The big difference between the Pop-Rocks-and-soda mixture and the vinegar–baking soda concoction is that the first combination doesn't create any new gas. Carbon dioxide gas was already trapped in the Pop Rocks' bubbles and the bubbles in the bottle of soda. This concoction produced a **physical change**, which is when a change occurs but it is not the result of a chemical reaction. In the case of the vinegar and baking soda, new carbon dioxide was created, which is a chemical change.

# Swimming Raisins

With the power of bubbles, you can turn a raisin into a wrinkled little Michael Phelps!

## Steps

1. Look at the liquid inside a closed bottle of clear soda or seltzer. Do you see any bubbles? Now open the bottle and pour some of the liquid into a tall, clear glass. Where did all the bubbles come from? Watch them travel up from the bottom of the glass.

2. Soon after pouring the soda or seltzer, drop five raisins into the glass. Watch the raisins carefully. Do they sink or float? Over the next few minutes, keep an eye on the raisins. What happens? Does this experiment work differently if you cut the raisins in half before you drop them in?

3. Repeat this experiment with chocolate chips, bits of uncooked angel hair pasta, or anything else you can think of that's about the same size.

4. Try this experiment another way: Make your own bubbles using baking soda and vinegar. Clean out the glass and fill it halfway with water. Add in about 2–3 teaspoons of baking soda and stir. Drop a few raisins in the glass, letting them sink to the bottom. Then *slowly* pour in some vinegar. What happened to the raisins?

### Stuff You Need

- 1 bottle of clear soda or seltzer
- raisins
- chocolate chips
- uncooked angel hair pasta (broken into little bits)
- water
- 2–3 teaspoons baking soda
- vinegar
- tall, clear glass
- measuring spoons
- a heaping helping of bat guano

## Hmmm... What's Going On?

Why did the raisins float and sink over and over again? Raisins are denser than soda, so they sink at first. But then the little carbon dioxide bubbles stick to the surfaces of the raisins and lift them up! When the raisins get to the top, the bubbles pop, releasing their carbon dioxide into the air. *Poof!* This makes the raisins sink down again. Eventually, the raisins absorb water, making them too dense for the carbon dioxide to lift, so they sit at the bottom.

I once tried this experiment with my Uncle Melvin's dandruff! It didn't work, but at least I got Uncle Melvin angry!

# Fizzy Eruption

THIS EXPERIMENT NEEDS AN ADULT MINION!

Normally, the gas bubbles in a bottle of soda escape gradually when you open it up. But using this experiment's trick, they come out very quickly and create a fizzy fountain!

**WARNING**: This concoction might give you a soda shower, so it's best to do it outside. Also, protect your eyes with goggles, dress in old clothes, and make sure a helpful grown-up is also dressed for mess!

## Stuff You Need

- ½ sheet white printer paper (8½ x 5½) OR large index card (5 x 8)
- 1 roll Mentos candy
- 2-liter bottle of diet soda at room temperature
- small stiff sheet of paper (like a playing card or business card)
- tape
- safety goggles
- paper towels

## Steps

TIP: Never try to do this experiment while piloting an airplane! Trust me, it doesn't work.

1. Create a Mentos launcher. This simple tool will allow you to drop all the candies quickly into the bottle at the same time. Put a half sheet of printer paper (or a large index card) on a flat surface. Place the package of Mentos at one of the shorter ends of the paper and roll the paper tightly around it. When it's all wrapped up in the paper tube, tape the tube to hold the shape. Then slide out the Mentos package.

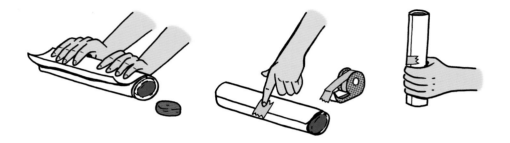

2. Go to an open outdoor area, away from others and anything that should stay dry. (If you are thinking, "Hey, we could do this in our living room!" or "Hey, let's put Dad's cell phone near the soda bottle!" then you'd better skip this experiment.) Oh, Jordan, you're such a party pooper!

3. Carefully take the cap off of a 2-liter bottle of room-temperature diet soda. Make sure the bottle is on flat, level ground so it won't tip over.

4. Put on safety goggles. Place a small stiff sheet of paper (like a playing card or business card) flat on top of the bottle opening.

5. Unwrap the Mentos candies, and load five of them into the paper tube. Put your finger over the bottom of the tube to prevent the candies from falling out.

6. Position the candy-filled tube over the stiff paper on the open soda bottle. Have your grown-up assistant make sure the bottle stays upright.

7. Tell anyone watching around you to stand back. When you're ready, count down from ten to one, then pull back the stiff paper so that all the Mentos slide into the soda bottle at the same time. Be careful not to tip the soda bottle over. Then step back yourself! Watch the amazing fountain of soda that shoots out of the bottle.

## Hmmm... What's Going On?

First, let's talk about how bubbles get into the soda bottle in the first place. At the factory, a special machine pumps lots of carbon dioxide into the sugary liquid in the bottle. Then another machine quickly screws on a cap to trap the gas inside. ~~Later, unless a sneaky mad scientist has just shaken the bottle (and, yes, Dr. Fickleschmutz, I'm talking about you)~~ the gas slowly escapes with that satisfying *sssssss* sound as the pressure is released when you open the bottle. If the bottle is shaken before it is opened, then the bubbles escape quickly, causing an overflow. This is because many of the tiny carbon dioxide bubbles from all parts of the bottle have been quickly moved to the empty space near the top of the bottle. When the bottle is opened, they all rush out at once.

Hey, I saw that!

So why did the Mentos candy cause the fizzy fountain? To understand the answer, you need to look closely at a single Mentos candy (the picture on the left). As you can see, the surface of this candy isn't perfectly smooth. It is covered with teeny-tiny craters. Since carbon dioxide tends to stick to solids, these little craters give the gas lots of places to stick to. In other words, the little bumps help the gas from the liquid escape very quickly—which causes the eruption. The neck of the bottle forces the soda upward, into a fountain.

A close-up view of a Mentos candy

## Silly Science Online: Fizzy Fountain Fiesta

Some folks take their Mentos–diet soda experiments very seriously. Go online and search for "extreme Mentos experiments." In one, you'll see what happens when you combine 200 liters of diet soda with over five hundred mints!

# Groovy Blobs in a Bottle

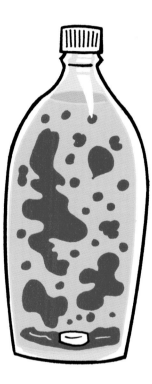

After you make this homemade version of a lava lamp, you'll see for yourself what happens when oil and water are put together.

*Jordan, you forgot to mention that this experiment should never ever be done at the top of the Eiffel Tower. Quel dommage!*

## Stuff You Need

- water
- 1 bottle of vegetable oil (check with a parent before you use up the whole thing!)
- food coloring (any color)
- 2 Alka-Seltzer tablets
- clear plastic bottle with a screw-on cap (such as a soda or water bottle)
- small plastic funnel
- large flashlight

## Steps

1. Fill a clear plastic bottle ¼ full with water.

2. Use a funnel to fill the rest of the bottle with vegetable oil, leaving about 2 inches of space near the top. Why do you think the water and oil didn't mix?

3. Drop in about 10 drops of food coloring, one drop at a time. Watch the drops as they travel down through the oil to the water level. What happened? Were you surprised that the drops didn't add color to the oil?

4. Break an Alka-Seltzer tablet into four chunks. Drop one in and observe what happens. What do you think is causing all those bubbles? After the bubbling stops, add the rest of the Alka-Seltzer chunks, one at a time.

5. Once all the bubbling has stopped, screw on the bottle cap and tilt the bottle back and forth to watch the blobs move about and join together.

6. Ready to take this experiment to the next level? Carefully place the bottle on top of the lens of a large flashlight, then unscrew the cap and add some additional chunks of Alka-Seltzer. With the lit-up colorful bubbles, the bottle looks like one of those groovy lava lamps from the 1960s!

# Hmmm... What's Going On?

Why don't oil and water mix? The short answer: Oil and water have different intermolecular forces. *Huh?* Hang on, I'll explain. **Intermolecular forces** are electromagnetic forces that keep molecules together in matter. But the forces that keep water molecules together are different from the forces that keep oil molecules together. In other words, molecules that make up water have a different polarity (charge) than the molecules that make up oil.

A **polar molecule** is one that has a positive charge on one end and a negative charge on the other. Think of polar molecules like little magnets, with a positive side and a negative side. Any chemical that is polar (such as water, salt, or sugar) will easily mix together with other polar chemicals. A **nonpolar molecule** has no charge. Any chemical that is nonpolar (such as oil, gasoline, or turpentine) will only mix together with other nonpolar substances. So because water (polar) and oil (nonpolar) have different charges, they won't mix.

*Oh, you mean like the sneaky charges I put on your credit card, Jordan?! C'mon, I need all those pogo sticks!*

# Chemistry Big Shot
# Robert Boyle (1627–1691)

Considered a founder of modern chemistry, **Robert Boyle** was one of the first scientists to use experiments to test out his ideas. He's most famous for his experiments on air, using an air pump that he invented. This tool could squeeze air into, or remove air from, closed containers. Using it, Boyle discovered that, if the amount and temperature of a gas are constant, when air pressure increases, the volume of air decreases. This is now known as Boyle's Law. If you want to see Boyle's Law in action, go on the Internet and search for "Boyle's Law video."

Robert Boyle

*Didn't you play in that heavy metal hair band the Sceptical Chymists back in the '80s? ~F.*

# COOL FACTS... Water

You can't tell by looking at it, but a glass of water is actually a concoction of sorts. The water contains a combination of two different gases (hydrogen and oxygen) that have joined to make a liquid. Even if you don't know a lot about chemistry, you may already know water's chemical formula: $H_2O$.

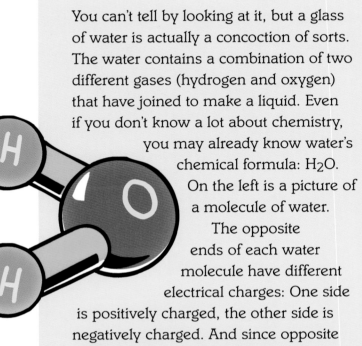

On the left is a picture of a molecule of water. The opposite ends of each water molecule have different electrical charges: One side is positively charged, the other side is negatively charged. And since opposite charges attract, water molecules are "sticky" and pull toward each other.

• Your body is almost 60 percent water. Your brain is made up of 70 percent water, and your lungs are almost 90 percent water. Given how important water is to your body, you need to drink a lot of it every day. And when you're exercising, don't wait until you feel thirsty to drink. Feeling thirsty is your body's way of warning you that you could become dehydrated, which could make you sick.

• Water is the only substance that is naturally found on Earth as a liquid, a solid (ice), *and* a gas (steam).

• Only 3 percent of Earth's water can be used as drinking water. 75 percent of the world's freshwater is frozen in the polar ice caps.

• There is the same amount of water on Earth today as there was when the Earth was formed. The glass of water you drink today could contain molecules that dinosaurs drank many millions of years ago.

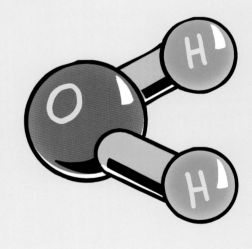

# CHAPTER 4

# Crazy Colors

Get ready for some colorful chemistry! In this chapter, you'll create concoctions that let you play with colors in surprising ways. Some of these experiments let you see how food coloring blends and moves when it's put into different liquids. You'll also whip up a special solution that will tell you if a liquid is an acid or a base. Let's get mixing!

Jordan, remember when I dropped your wallet in fluorosulfuric acid? Wasn't that HILARIOUS?!
-F.

# Milky Rainbow Burst

Sure, soap is wonderful for washing your hands. But did you know it can also help you create a blast of beautiful colors in your kitchen?

*Speaking of colors, Jordan, remember when I put all those cherries and blueberries in a blender in your kitchen? I guess I should have put the top on the blender— I'm soooo forgetful sometimes.*

## Steps

1. Pour milk into a plate with raised edges so it completely covers the bottom. Wait a few minutes to let the milk settle.

2. Squeeze about 5–10 drops of one color of food coloring near the center of the milk on the plate. Repeat this with a second color near the first color, but not on top of it. Then do the same with the third and fourth colors.

3. Squeeze a small amount of dishwashing soap in the small cup and swirl a cotton swab in it.

4. Carefully place the cotton swab with the soap on it in a milk-only spot in the middle of the plate. Hold it there, and don't move it around.

   Now remove the swab. What happened to the colors on the plate?

6. Dip another cotton swab in the soap and put the tip in another place on the plate. In which direction do the colors move? What do you think is happening?

7. If you have other kinds of milk around (such as buttermilk or skim milk), repeat this experiment to see how the different fat contents of the milks affect the results.

## Hmmm... What's Going On?

What's the special connection between soap and milk? Milk looks like it is made up of only one thing—a white liquid. But it actually contains tiny droplets of fat, proteins, vitamins, and minerals.

Normally, the little blobs of fat are kept apart from one another. When you added the dish soap, this weakened the chemical bonds that kept these fats apart. The fat molecules moved as quickly as possible to connect with other fat molecules. Since the food coloring (which is made of mostly water) got in the way of the fat molecules moving, the colors were pushed this way and that, quickly spreading out like colorful fireworks.

The fat globules stick together because they are nonpolar, and the food coloring is polar. In other words, they have different charges. The dish soap breaks up the fat droplets into even tinier fat droplets, which then are attracted to other teeny fat droplets. Soap works because it has both polar and nonpolar chemicals in it. The nonpolar chemicals dissolve nonpolar things (like grease, oil, and fat) while the polar parts dissolve polar things and allow the grease, oil, and fat to also dissolve in water.

**Talk Like a Scientist**

*blah, blah, blah...*

**COLLOID**

What do milk, glue, your blood, and gooey glop (see page 13) have in common? They're all colloids. A **colloid** is a mixture whose molecules aren't fully combined. When you stir salt into a glass of water, the salt dissolves into and combines with the water. But in a colloid, the substances don't combine; they mix together, but some of the particles keep their characteristics. For instance, in the case of milk, most of the liquid is water, but throughout the water are teeny-tiny droplets of fat. These bits of fat aren't big enough to be pulled down by gravity, so they stay suspended in the mixture.

Hey, that reminds me! I have to remember to call Lloyd. He's my personal hair stylist. Geez, the upkeep on the whole mad scientist look is very time-consuming.

# Color Breakthrough

**How does food coloring act in water (a polar liquid) versus oil (a nonpolar liquid)? Let's find out!**

## Steps

1. Fill a plastic cup full of water. Put in drops of two different colors of food coloring, not letting the drops touch. What happens? Stir the water for about ten seconds. What does the water look like now?

2. Fill a different cup ⅔ full with water, then add vegetable oil until the cup is almost full. Now repeat what you did with the different colored drops of food coloring. What happens?

   TIP: It is important to keep the cups as still as possible as you put in the drops.

3. Use a sharpened pencil to push down one of the drops of food coloring through the oil-water mixture. What happens?

4. Now sprinkle some salt on top of the cup with the oil and food coloring. What happens to the oil?

## Hmmm... What's Going On?

Food coloring is made mostly of water, so when it is dropped into plain water, it easily "joins the team" and spreads out quickly. But oil and water don't mix! Water molecules like to stick together, so they push oil molecules out of the way. When you drop the food coloring in the oil, each little blob of food coloring is wrapped in oil, so it stays by itself, like a little island in an ocean. When you poke the color blob with a pencil, the oil layer is broken—and the food coloring can escape to the water layer and spread out. Why did things start moving when salt was sprinkled on top? Salt is even more polar than water. In other words, it has stronger positive and negative charges. Once the salt dissolves in the water, the water molecules "want" to stick together even more, and push away the oil molecules that get in their way.

## Stuff You Need

- water
- food coloring (in two colors)
- vegetable oil
- table salt
- 3 clear plastic cups
- spoon
- sharpened pencil

1/4 teaspoon of that crusty stuff found in your eyes when you wake up

# Chemistry Big Shot
## Carl Scheele (1742–1786)

Take a deep breath. Most of the air you just inhaled is made of two invisible gases, nitrogen (78 percent) and oxygen (21 percent). **Carl W. Scheele** (SHAY-leh), a clever chemist in the early 1770s, discovered the second of these gases. Before Scheele's discovery, scientists thought there were two kinds of air: one kind that keeps fires going ("fire air"), and one that does not ("foul air").

To get pure oxygen, Scheele did countless experiments. Sometimes, he would mix strong acids together and trap the gases that were released. Other times, he would heat up toxic chemicals and study the fumes.

Scheele became wildly interested in experimenting with chemicals as a teenager, when he worked in a pharmacy. Not having the proper science equipment didn't stop him. He created complicated experiments with homemade tools, including the preserved bladder of an ox!

So what? I created noxious gases by mixing bean dip with sauerkraut juice at dinner! P-U!
~F.

If you want to recreate Scheele's experiment at home, I know a guy who sells ox bladders super cheap. His Web site is www.getyouroxbladdersherenow.com Tell 'em, Dr. Fickleschmutz sent you.

# Am I Blue?

One moment the solution is clear, and the next it's blue. Then, like magic, it's clear again. You'll think you're seeing things!

## Steps

1. Put on safety goggles. Pour 1 cup of water into a saucepan and, with a grown-up's help, heat it on the stove over medium heat. Add 1 teaspoon of cornstarch and stir it until it dissolves.

2. Use the oven mitts to help you remove the pan from the heat and set it on a heat-safe surface. Then add 1 more cup of water and ½ cup of hydrogen peroxide. Use the medicine dropper to add 5 drops of white vinegar to this mixture. Stir well.

## Stuff You Need

- 2 cups water
- 1 teaspoon cornstarch
- 3% hydrogen peroxide (available at a pharmacy)
- white vinegar
- 2 drops tincture of iodine (available at a pharmacy)
- 1 teaspoon baking powder
- safety goggles
- measuring spoons
- measuring cup
- saucepan
- stove
- oven mitts
- spoon
- medicine dropper (available at pharmacy)
- rubber gloves (optional: to avoid getting iodine stains on your hands)
- clear drinking glass

TIP: Put on rubber gloves if you have them. They'll help you avoid any iodine stains on your skin. If you don't have them, just be careful and make sure to wash your hands well after the next step.

3. Don't put your fingers near your mouth or eyes while doing this step! Clean out the medicine dropper with water, and use it to add 2 drops of tincture of iodine to the bottom of the drinking glass. Be careful not to spill any of the iodine, as it stains easily.

4. Have your grown-up helper carefully pour the solution from the pan into the clear glass. What happens to the color of the liquid?

5. Sprinkle in 1 teaspoon of baking powder. Wait at least 10 seconds. What happens to the color now?

6. Put exactly seven ice cubes down your best friend's shirt. Why? Because Dr. Fickleschmutz says so.

## Hmmm... What's Going On?

The color change in this experiment happens because any kind of starch (like cornstarch) has a reaction when mixed with iodine and turns blue. The starch molecules are natural polymers that spiral. The iodine gets caught in the spiral and forms a "complex" with the starch, which has an intense color. It is called a complex because we have something new, but the iodine still retains its structure and the starch retains its structure—they are attracted by intermolecular forces.

You can try this out in the kitchen by putting drops of iodine on foods that have starch in them, such as potatoes, rice, pasta, bread, and flour. If you drop iodine on non-starchy foods, such as a fresh cucumber or salt, it won't turn them blue.

The baking powder turned the solution clear again because of what scientists call a reverse reaction. The molecules in the baking powder undid the effect of the original iodine-starch reaction.

# Acid or Base? The Cabbage Knows!

You're about to make cabbage juice! Don't worry, you're not going to drink it. You are going to use it to do some chemistry detective work.

*Speak for yourself, Jordan. I'm quite fond of red cabbage-garlic-prune smoothies! I usually down a big C.G.P. smoothie first thing in the morning.*

## Stuff You Need

- 2–3 cups water
- 4 red cabbage leaves
- white vinegar
- laundry detergent
- lemon juice
- can or bottle of soda
- Alka-Seltzer tablet
- safety goggles
- blender
- large bowl
- strainer
- 5 clear drinking glasses (or clear cups)
- spoon

**WARNING:** Cabbage juice can stain! So suit up in some old clothes, protect your eyes with goggles, and get your grown-up helper to do the same!

## Steps

1. Put on safety goggles. With a grown-up's help, fill a blender halfway with water (2–3 cups). Peel off and break up four red cabbage leaves, then stick them in the blender. Cover and blend on high for about a minute. Voilà! You have a batch of cabbage juice.

2. In the sink, place a large bowl beneath a strainer. Then pour the cabbage mixture through the strainer, catching all the purple liquid in the bowl.

3. Put two clear drinking glasses next to each other and fill each one halfway with cabbage juice.

*True story: When I was a kid, I gave my younger brother a glass of clear liquid and told him, "Drink it, Wolfgang! It will make you smarter!" He took one sip, spit it out, and said, "Yeech! That's vinegar!" And I said, "See? You're getting smarter!"*

THIS EXPERIMENT NEEDS AN ADULT MINION!

52

Ah, that's just the fuel I use to make LOTS of gas!!

4. Now pour a little white vinegar into the first glass of cabbage juice. Stir with a spoon. What happens?

5. In the second glass, add a teaspoon of laundry detergent to the cabbage juice. What happens?

6. Fill three more empty glasses halfway with the purple cabbage juice. Add one of each of the remaining ingredients to these glasses—lemon juice, a soft drink, and an Alka-Seltzer tablet. Look carefully at the color of each glass's liquid. What does it mean?

## Hmmm... What's Going On?

Cabbage juice is what scientists call an indicator. It contains anthocyanin, which changes color when it's mixed with an acid or a base. Acids and bases are materials that conduct electricity but have opposite charges. An **acidic solution** has excess hydrogen ions (H+), while a **basic solution** has excess hydroxide ions (OH-). Acids, such as lemon juice and vinegar, tend to have a sour taste. Bases, such as ammonia, baking soda, and cleaning bleach, tend to have a slippery feel. Pure water is neutral—it is neither acidic nor basic. Scientists use a tool called the pH scale from 0 to 14 to measure acids and bases.

When the hydrogen ions in an acid react with the cabbage juice, a chemical reaction occurs that turns the juice red. When the hydroxide ions in a base mix with the cabbage juice, it changes to green or blue.

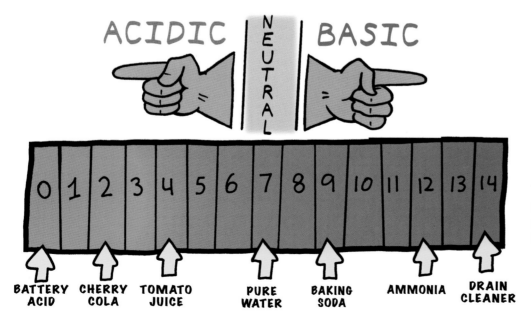

The stronger an acid is, the closer it is to 0 on the scale. The stronger a base is, the closer to 14 it is.

# THE DISCOVERY OF POST-ITS

A chemist named Spencer Silver was working in his lab in 1970. He was trying to invent a new type of glue for his company, 3M. When he put this glue on two pieces of paper, he found that it was very weak and the pieces of paper could be easily pulled apart. Silver told other scientists about it—but no one saw a purpose for it. Then, four years later, one of the scientist's friends was singing in the church choir and was faced with a problem: Every time he put paper bookmarks in his songbook, they fell out. If only he had some gentle glue that wouldn't damage the pages… Aha! His friend Spencer's "failed" glue would be perfect for the bookmarking job. Today, Post-its are super popular, are sold by the billions, and are found in many offices, schools, and homes.

# CHEMISTRY BIG SHOT

## DR. VISKUS VON FICKLESCHMUTZ (1932-   )

As a boy in Bnozgzerkurplanzd, young Viskus dreamed of one day becoming a world-famous, superbrilliant GENIUS. His teachers laughed and said he was crazy, which was totally ridiculous, and they were just jealous, and who cares what they think, anyway? The important thing: He stuck to this goal! Today, Fickleschmutz's remarkable intelligence, stunning good looks, and musical flatulence skills have made him a living legend in the scientific community. His famous concoctions include bacon-scented perfume, banana-sardine smoothies, and spray socks. Today, he writes science books for kids (both children and goats). His hobbies include mooing to opera, cockroach taxidermy, and, of course, hopscotch.

# CHAPTER 5

# Incredible and Edible

Cooking is all about chemistry. Every time you make cookies and pop them in the oven, you're making lots of chemical reactions. Up until now, the safety rules of this book have warned you against putting any of the experiments in your mouth. This chapter is the exception. Every project is meant to be tasted once it's finished. So happy experimenting and bon appetit!

**IF YOU HAVE FOOD ALLERGIES:** Before you put any mixture in your mouth, make sure that it does not contain any foods that you are allergic to.

I love to cook, too, Jordan! My specialty: beetle grub goulash! (Garnished with fresh toenail clippings.) Yum! —F.

# It Jiggles! It Glows!

**What's that jiggling, glowing thing on the table? Oh, it's dessert.**

Look! It's Mt. Wiggle-manjaro! She's gonna blow!

## Stuff You Need

- nonstick spray
- 1 cup tap water
- 1 cup cold tonic water
- 1 package of blue or green Jell-O or other brand of flavored gelatin
- rectangular mold OR glass pan
- saucepan
- stove
- oven mitts
- wooden spoon
- cookie cutters (optional)
- cookie sheet with edges OR sink (to fill with warm water to loosen set gelatin)
- black light (available in hardware stores, costume shops, or online)

## Steps

1. Spray your mold or glass pan with nonstick spray.

2. Pour 1 cup of tap water into a saucepan. With a grown-up's help, bring it to a boil on the stove.

3. Using oven mitts, take the pot off the stove and set it on a heat-safe surface. Stir in the gelatin powder with a wooden spoon until completely dissolved (about two minutes).

4. Stir in 1 cup of cold tonic water. Pour into your lightly sprayed mold or glass pan.

5. Refrigerate until the gelatin has set (about four hours).

6. If you'd like, cut the gelatin into shapes using cookie cutters. Rest the bottom of the pan or mold in some warm water, in either a sink or a cookie sheet with edges. This will loosen the gelatin. Then remove the cutouts or flip the gelatin over onto a serving plate.

7. In a dark room, shine a black light on the gelatin to make it glow.

8. If you want your gelatin to really glow, stick it inside a nuclear reactor!

## Hmmm... What's Going On?

The secret stuff that makes this Jell-O glow in the black light is quinine. That's one of the ingredients in tonic water. Quinine is a chemical that comes from the bark of the cinchona tree. In the 1600s, people discovered that quinine helped treat a terrible disease called malaria. By putting quinine in tonic water, scientists were able to help fight malaria in India and Africa. Quinine is similar to some of the chemicals used in sunscreen. These chemicals, like quinine, absorb the UV light and keep your skin from absorbing it.

Black light gives off one kind of light we can see (visible light) and another we cannot. The light that is invisible to our eyes is ultraviolet light (sometimes called UV light). When tonic water is put under a black light, the quinine in the tonic water absorbs the UV light. This energizes the quinine's electrons. (**Electrons** are the itty-bitty, invisible particles that move around the outside of an atom.) These excited electrons give off their extra energy as blue light (depending on the Jell-O color).

**Peter Cooper**

JELL-O FOR BRAINS! -F.

## The Story Behind... Jell-O

In the 1800s, New York businessman **Peter Cooper** came up with all sorts of interesting inventions, including the first American-built steam-powered train, the *Tom Thumb*. But his jiggliest invention, without question, was Jell-O. He didn't call it that, and he didn't actually invent the idea of gelatin. The idea of boiling animal bones to get gelatin had been around for many years. What Cooper did was figure out how to manufacture a gelatin dessert. He didn't make much money from this idea, so he sold it to Pearl B. Wait, a cough syrup manufacturer in 1895. Wait's wife, May, came up with the catchy name "Jell-O"—but they, too, didn't make any money from it. So the Waits sold the idea to their neighbor Orator Francis Woodward. This guy spent lots of money advertising it, and was crafty, too. He advertised Jell-O as "America's Most Famous Dessert"—even though most people had never heard of it! By 1906, the sales reached one million dollars. Today, more than three hundred million boxes of Jell-O are sold every year.

# Secret Message Muffins

**THIS EXPERIMENT NEEDS AN ADULT MINION!**

*Psst…* There is more to these muffins than meets the eye! Not only are they loaded with yummy ingredients, but buried inside each tasty muffin is a mysterious message.

*What?! Jordan, you stole this recipe from my secret files! It was invented by great-great-grandpa Max Stoopnagle, who was a spy in Flegsnimenthal, Latvia. He even once used one of these muffins to propose marriage to my great-great-grandma Bloozabella. A lovely lady, she was, except her stuffed cabbage tasted like sewage...*

## Stuff You Need

- ballpoint pen
- twenty-four 1" x 2½" inch pieces of paper
- aluminum foil, cut into small pieces to wrap the messages, each about 1½" x 3"
- 1 cup all-purpose flour
- 1 cup oat bran
- 1 teaspoon baking soda
- 1 teaspoon baking powder
- 2 tablespoons unsweetened cocoa
- 2 teaspoons lemon juice
- ½ cup milk
- 1 cup butter
- ½ cup granulated sugar
- 2 eggs, lightly beaten
- 1 teaspoon vanilla extract
- 3 medium mashed ripe bananas (about 1 cup total)
- 1 cup chocolate chips
- oven
- muffin pan
- paper muffin cups
- measuring spoons
- measuring cups
- 2 medium bowls
- small bowl
- mixing spoon

## Steps

1. Use a ballpoint pen to write secret messages on twenty-four little pieces of paper. Roll up the messages into little scrolls, wrap them in pieces of aluminum foil, and set them aside.

2. Preheat oven to 350°F. Line a muffin pan with paper cups.

3. In a medium bowl, mix together the dry ingredients: flour, oat bran, baking soda, baking powder, and unsweetened cocoa.

4. In a small bowl, stir the lemon juice into the milk.

5. In another medium bowl, cream the butter and sugar together, then add the eggs, vanilla, and mashed bananas.

6. Add the milk and banana mixtures into the bowl with the dry ingredients. Mix just until moistened. Don't overmix.

7. Spoon batter into the muffin cups until they're about ⅔ full.

8. Stick a rolled-up message into each muffin so it sticks halfway out the top.

9. Place a few chocolate chips on the top of each muffin. *And put 23 chips in your mouth!*

10. Bake for 20–25 minutes. Remove from oven with oven mitts, and let cool before tasting.

## Hmmm... What's Going On?

What makes these muffins rise in the oven? The power of carbon dioxide strikes again! Did you wonder why you were asked to mix all the dry ingredients together first—before adding them to the wet ones? That's because one of the dry ingredients—baking soda—starts making carbon dioxide as soon as it's wet. When the baking soda mixes with the lemon juice and the egg, chemical reactions take place. The heat of the oven also helps the bubbles in the batter rise up. The other liquid ingredients are there to add flavor and texture to the muffins.

# The Fastest Chocolate Cake Ever

THIS EXPERIMENT NEEDS AN ADULT MINION!

TIP: Don't eat the candle!

If you love chocolate cake, but don't have time to bake a whole cake, you're in luck. This tasty, single-serving cake can be whipped up in about five minutes.

## Stuff You Need

- 4 tablespoons cake flour
  **NOTE:** If you can't find cake flour, you can make your own by mixing 1¾ cups of all-purpose flour with ¼ cup of cornstarch and sifting this mixture several times.
- 4 tablespoons sugar
- 2 tablespoons cocoa
- 2 tablespoons whisked egg
- 3 tablespoons milk
- 3 tablespoons oil
- ¼ teaspoon vanilla extract
- 3 tablespoons chocolate chips
- microwave-safe mug
- bowl
- fork
- spoon
- microwave oven
- plate
- oven mitts
- ice cream (optional)

## Steps

1. Mix the dry ingredients (cake flour, sugar, and cocoa) in a microwave-safe mug. Crack an egg into a bowl, whisk it with a fork, then stir 2 tablespoons of the egg into the other ingredients.

2. Pour in the milk, oil, vanilla extract, and chocolate chips, and mix it all together.

3. With help from a grown-up, put the mug in the microwave (set on high) for 3 minutes.

4. Watch through the microwave window. Wait until the mixture inside the mug stops rising and settles. Using oven mitts, remove the mug from the microwave and put it on a heat-safe surface.

5. Let the cake cool completely (about 5–10 minutes).

6. Have your grown-up helper test to make sure the mug has cooled. Then use a spoon or dull knife to gently tip the contents of the mug onto a plate.

7. Eat! Serve with ice cream if you wish.

## Hmmm... What's Going On?

Why are most cakes not baked in microwave ovens? As you've discovered from this experiment, a microwave cake isn't as fluffy as the kind you could create in a normal oven. One reason is that microwaves simply aren't hot enough to turn cake batter chemicals into yummy cake.

In a regular oven, cakes are usually baked at 350°F. This hot temperature allows a bunch of chemical reactions to take place. Ingredients are bonded, solid fats melt, proteins change shape, gases are formed or released, and so on. Microwaves, on the other hand, use radio waves to cook food. These tiny electromagnetic waves bounce around billions of times a second! All the friction of the water molecules zooming back and forth heats up the water, fats, and sugars inside the food. But the temperatures in a microwave never get hot enough to "cook" the food. They only heat up the water molecules in the food. Microwave heating is uneven, which is why microwave ovens have spinning trays. Foods can't burn in a microwave the way they do in an oven; they just get hard as the water is driven out.

Speaking of radio, try WFKL: All Fickleschmutz, All the Time!

Did you wonder why this recipe asked you to use cake flour rather than regular flour? Cake flour is lighter, since it has been chopped more finely in the factory. It also contains more starch, so it can hold more fat and sugar without collapsing. Cake flour has a lower protein content than regular flour. That's a good thing because the more protein flour has, the more gluten will be produced when it's baked. And the more gluten that is produced, the more chewy the cake's texture will be.

# The Story Behind . . .
# Sugar

If you're like most people, you *love* sugar! The average American eats about 45 pounds of it a year. Where does sugar come from? Yes, I know, the supermarket. But what about before that? The sugar you eat started off as a plant that looked like the picture on the left: That's sugarcane. It grows in warm, tropical countries and can grow to be 12 feet tall. After being chopped down with a long sharp sword, it's taken to a factory where it is shredded and pressed. Carbon dioxide is added to the sugar cane juice, and it is boiled until it becomes a thick syrup. This syrup is left out until all the water evaporates. As the water leaves the liquid, it leaves behind sugar crystals. These crystals are spun in a big spinning machine called a centrifuge (kind of like a big washing machine). The liquid is again pushed out, leaving behind wet, brown raw sugar. It's not edible yet, though. It's sent to another factory where it is washed, purified, boiled, evaporated, and allowed to crystallize again.

Oops! This page made me hungry for a chocolate bar!

63

## ARTIFICIAL SWEETENER

What is one hundred and sixty times sweeter than sugar? The answer is aspartame, a chemical that is often used to sweeten diet soda and other food products. It's sold under trademarked names such as NutraSweet and Equal. Like Silly Putty and Post-it notes, aspartame was invented by accident. In 1965, a chemist named James Schlatter was working for a company that was trying to develop a medicine to treat ulcers. (Ulcers are a painful condition that can affect the lining of the stomach.) While Schlatter was mixing chemicals one day, he spilled some of them on the outside of the glass container he was using. Later, he accidentally licked his fingers and tasted something very sweet. He figured out it was the aspartame.

*Whenever this guy dropped test tubes in his lab, you know what he called it? A Schlattersplatter!*

*What two gases make up your STINKY BREATH? It makes my EYES water! ~F.*

## Chemistry Big Shot
## Antoine Lavoisier (1743–1794)

Often called the father of modern chemistry, **Antoine Lavoisier** is famous for his Law of Conservation of Mass. This scientific idea says that if you weigh all the chemicals at the start of a reaction, and then weigh them again at the end, you'll find that their total weight is the same. By doing careful experiments, he discovered that the air we breathe is made mostly of two gases, nitrogen and oxygen. He also discovered that water is made of two elements, oxygen and hydrogen. Despite his brilliant discoveries, he never achieved one of his life goals— to discover a new element.

# Sour Milk Biscuits

THIS EXPERIMENT NEEDS AN ADULT MINION!

When you hear the words *sour* and *milk* together, you might think *Yeeech!* But mixing in some homemade sour milk to these biscuits makes them delicious.

## Steps

1. First, you have to make some sour milk. Pour ½ cup of whole milk into a small bowl and let it warm up to room temperature. This should take about 30–40 minutes. You can use a thermometer to measure the temperature of the milk and compare it with temperature of the room.

   **IMPORTANT:** I'm *not* talking about leaving out a bowl of milk until it spoils and smells horrible. Drinking that kind of milk could make you very sick. So don't do it!

2. Put 2 teaspoons of vinegar into another small bowl. Pour the milk into the vinegar and stir. Wait for 10 minutes. You now have sour milk!

3. Preheat the oven to 450°F.

### Stuff You Need

- ½ cup whole milk, room temperature
- 2 teaspoons vinegar
- 1 cup flour
- 1 teaspoon baking powder
- ⅛ teaspoon baking soda
- ½ teaspoon salt
- 2 tablespoons butter
- measuring spoons
- measuring cups
- 2 small bowls
- spoon
- oven
- medium bowl
- hand pastry blender OR 2 butter knives
- fork
- cookie sheet
- parchment paper (optional)

# COOL FACTS... Salt

- Our blood is filled with salt. Without it, our brains and muscles wouldn't work properly. But don't eat too much salty food, or you could get sick.

- Table salt is made up of two chemicals called sodium and chlorine. Sodium and chlorine are both elements. By themselves, these chemicals are poisonous, but when they chemically react together, they make a completely new chemical that is safe to eat.

- Long ago, salt was considered so valuable that it was used as money. In fact, in the Middle Ages, salt was so expensive that it was sometimes referred to as white gold.

- Salt is the only rock we eat.

What do you call salty bread? Rock 'n' roll!

4. In a medium bowl, mix together the dry ingredients: flour, baking powder, baking soda, salt.

5. Using a pastry blender or two butter knives, cut in the butter until it looks like crumbs the size of small peas. (If you're using two knives, hold one in each hand pointing downward, cross your hands in the bowl, and pull the knives apart in opposite directions through the mixture. As the middle of the two knives touch, you'll gently chop and blend the ingredients.)

6. Add the sour milk and stir with a fork until all the ingredients are combined.

7. Put spoonfuls of dough onto an ungreased cookie sheet.

   **TIP:** To prevent the biscuits from sticking, you can put a sheet of parchment paper on the cookie sheet before you put down the dough.

8. Bake for 12–15 minutes until golden brown.

## Hmmm... What's Going On?

How does mixing vinegar in the milk help this recipe taste better? The acid in the vinegar "denatures" the proteins in the milk. This means it messes with the protein's chemical structure.

What's the difference between baking soda and baking powder? As you may know, both powders help a cake or bread to rise. When they are heated up, they create carbon dioxide bubbles that make the dough rise. Baking soda also creates sodium carbonate in this chemical reaction, and it doesn't taste good. Baking powder is actually baking soda with some acid added in. This acid helps use up the sodium carbonate, so the food tastes less bitter.

# Easy Chilly Pickle Slices

THIS EXPERIMENT NEEDS AN ADULT MINION!

This concoction will turn unsuspecting cucumbers into tasty pickles! To get really flavorful pickles, you have to wait a few days. But if you're patient, you'll be able to crunch into your delicious creations.

*Last night, I had a wacky dream that I was running through the streets in my underpants. Then I discovered, it wasn't a dream — I was sleepwalking. Talk about being in a pickle! (You knew there was a reason I was telling you this story, right?)*

## Stuff You Need

- 1 seedless cucumber OR 6 Kirby cucumbers (sometimes called pickling cucumbers)
- 2 cups water
- 1¾ cups white vinegar
- 1½ cups fresh dill weed, chopped
- ½ cup sugar
- 8 cloves garlic, peeled and sliced
- 1½ tablespoons kosher salt
- 1 tablespoon pickling spice (available in the spice aisle at the supermarket)
- sharp knife
- cutting board
- medium bowl
- mixing spoon
- plastic wrap
- plastic or glass container with lid OR ziplock freezer bags (thicker plastic than a regular ziplock bag)

## Steps

1. With help from an adult, carefully slice the cucumber(s) into thin slices with a sharp knife.

2. In a medium bowl, mix together the sliced cucumbers, water, white vinegar, chopped dill, sugar, sliced garlic, kosher salt, and pickling spice. Stir, cover with plastic wrap, and let stand at room temperature for 2 hours, until the sugar and salt have dissolved.

# COOL FACTS...
## Vinegar

- The word *vinegar* comes from the French words *vin* ("wine") and *aigre* ("sour").

- Vinegar is called acetic acid by scientists. Its chemical formula is $CH_3COOH$.

- Any liquid that has sugar or starch in it will eventually turn to vinegar when it is exposed to air. People have made vinegar from raspberries, rice, and even bananas.

- If you go to Roslyn, South Dakota, you can visit the International Vinegar Museum, run by Lawrence Diggs, who calls himself (what else?) the Vinegar Man.

- In 400 B.C., Hippocrates, the man referred to as the father of medicine, used to treat some of his patients with vinegar. He'd give it to them to treat everything from allergies to infected wounds.

3. Pour the cucumbers and liquid into a plastic or glass container with a lid, or a ziplock freezer bag tightly sealed, and put in the refrigerator. Give the container or bag a good shake every day.

4. Wait. This is the hard part, I know.

5. In about 4–5 days, taste your pickles. Enjoy! The pickles will keep for a couple weeks. If you notice that the pickles give off a strange odor, or look spoiled, toss them immediately.

## Hmmm... What's Going On?

Vinegar is an acid. Acids cause foods to ferment. By placing the cucumber slices in the vinegar-salt solution, you are helping the fermentation. When you ferment a food, you encourage "good" bacteria to grow on it, while preventing "bad" bacteria from causing it to spoil. When a vegetable is soaked in a salt brine, this allows the growth of bacteria that eat the vegetable's sugars and produce tart-tasting lactic acid.

Long ago, before there were modern refrigerators, pickling was one of the main ways that people preserved vegetables so they could be enjoyed when they were out of season. People pickle all sorts of things, like peppers, eggs, asparagus, pigs' feet, and peaches.

THIS EXPERIMENT NEEDS AN ADULT MINION!

# Create Your Own Concoctions

Up until now, all the concoctions in this book have been based on formulas that have been carefully tested. In other words, you've been following in the slime-covered footprints of other mad scientists. Now it's time to take things into your own hands! Yes, it's time to invent your own marvelous mixtures! To help you get started, I've come up with a bunch of Crazy Concoction Challenges. For each one, I'll give you the basic rules— but the rest is up to you! So gather your ingredients, get mixing, and go for it!

Some in MY lab, which I had to clean up, with no help from you, Jordan!

Finally!! A chance for the readers to get out of control!!!

-F.

# CHAPTER 6

# Be SILLY, Be SAFE

**IMPORTANT:** Before you take any of the Crazy Concoction Challenges, look again at the safety guidelines on pages 10 and 11. In particular, make sure you have a grown-up with you when you embark on these chemistry adventures. The wonders of science are a lot more enjoyable when you don't have an adult screaming, "You mixed WHAT with WHAT in our kitchen?!" Plus, if you're really nice, I'll bet they'll help you clean up.

Pretending to be a mad scientist can be great fun, but don't really lose your mind while experimenting. If some bizarre concoction idea seems dangerous to you, DON'T DO IT.

*What are you implying here?! I'm just as sane as the next guy!*

**IF YOU HAVE FOOD ALLERGIES:** Some of these experiments involve tasting your concoctions. Before you put any mixture in your mouth, make sure that it does not contain any foods that you are allergic to.

KA-PLU-EE!!!

HA-HA!!
-F.

## CHALLENGE 1
# Mystery Mixture

Give yourself exactly two minutes to gather ten random ingredients from your kitchen. They can be anything, as long as they are safe—and okay with the adult helping you. Some suggestions: flour, cornstarch, ketchup, dish soap, corn syrup, egg, chopped ice, colored sprinkles, apple juice, spices such as oregano or garlic powder.

Now mix the **same small amount** (1 tablespoon, for example) of any five of these ingredients in a bowl. On a piece of paper, write down the names of the ingredients as you add them.

Find another mad scientist to play the mystery mixture challenge. This person's job is to carefully examine your completed mixture and figure out which five of the ten ingredients you used to make it. The guesser can ask you questions as they try to track down the answer. Every time he or she makes a correct guess, that ingredient is set aside, until all five have been collected.

**IMPORTANT:** Since some of the ingredients may not be edible (such as dish soap), make sure to tell your friend *not* to taste it.

Finally, to test out if their prediction is correct, the guesser mixes the five ingredients in a different bowl (using the same amount of each) and compares them to your bowl. Observe carefully. Do they match? Afterward, challenge the other mad scientist to make up a mystery mixture for you to solve.

# Talk Like a Scientist

*blah, blah, blah...*

# The Scientific Method

Scientists love to come up with interesting questions about how the world works. The **scientific method** is the careful, step-by-step way they search for answers. To follow this method, first you have to make some observations that lead you to a question. Examples: What type of bubble gum makes the largest bubbles? Why did that shampoo turn your sister's hair green? What will happen when you mix Ingredient A with Ingredient B?

Second, you have to come up with a hypothesis. A **hypothesis** is an educated guess about the answer to your question. It's more than a random guess. It is a smart guess based on what you already know. For example, if your question is
*How quickly will an ice cube melt?*
your hypothesis might be
*An ice cube will melt in twenty minutes.*

In order to test your hypothesis, you'll have to make decisions about various variables, or conditions. Will you test this outside on a hot summer day? Or inside a refrigerator?

Third, you have to do your experiment, writing down all the information you collect and observe. This information is called data. Often, you'll have to do an experiment many times to make sure you always get the same results.

Lastly, you make a conclusion to decide if your hypothesis is correct or not. Sometimes even the smartest scientists discover that their hypotheses weren't right, and they have to come up with new hypotheses and test them. And so on...

# Make a "Muck-Shake"

Your mission is simple: Create the most disgusting, awful-tasting mixture imaginable. The catch is that *you* have to be the tester. With a grown-up's help, pour about a cup of some drinkable liquid, such as milk or orange juice, into a blender. Then add in at least three more *edible* ingredients that should never go together. For example, tuna fish, chocolate syrup, and lemon juice; or bananas, lima beans, and peppermint ice cream. Next, whirl it all together in the blender. If it doesn't look gross enough, then try adding a few drops of food coloring.

Finally, the yuckiest part: Take a *small* sip! Have your grown-up get a camera ready and take your picture just as you take that little sip. It will be a classic for sure. Maybe you can persuade your grown-up to take a sip, too, and you can take a picture of him or her.

Hey, don't mock my favorite sandwich: a B.L.P.!

# Alphabetical Smoothie!

While most of Dr. Fickleschmutz's off-the-wall concoctions were too crazy for this book, he has an unusual talent for making smoothies. Give the guy a blender, and he would whip up wild mixtures that would make Willy Wonka say, "Whoa! I never thought of that!" When I visited his lab, he gave me this challenge: Pick a letter of the alphabet and gather several tasty ingredients that start with that letter. The trick is to pick ingredients that will taste great together. Then put them in a blender with some ice cubes and see what you come up with! If you pick A, you might combine apples, allspice, and apricots. If you pick C, maybe chocolate, cinnamon, and coffee ice cream! What do you think is the most delicious letter of the alphabet?

Hey, Jordan! Don't make me shampoo you with guacamole again.

# Sticky Stuff

What is the stickiest mixture you can invent? To find out, start with some famous sticky ingredients, such as peanut butter, honey, or caramel sauce, then add anything else you can think of. You will not be eating this mixture, so don't worry about combining strange tastes. The main rule is that the items in the mixture have to be *food*—no squeezing in glue.

Rub this stuff all over your grown-up partner's head! (But don't blame Dr. F if you get in trouble. Which you will.)

To test the sticky factor, spread a spoonful of this mixture on a plastic, disposable plate and leave it out for 5–6 hours, until it starts to harden. See if you can figure out how to remove this concoction from the plate using hot water, soap, scrubbing, and so on.

## CHALLENGE 5

# A Little of This, A Little of That

This concoction is all about mixing together spices. You know, things like garlic powder, oregano, and cinnamon. Get a little bowl and put in about 1 teaspoon of at least five different spices—the more, the better. Then add in one cup of flour and mix it all together. Finally, pour in about ¼ cup of oil and ¼ cup of water. Gush it all up with your hands, and smell all the weird scents blending together (but don't eat it!).

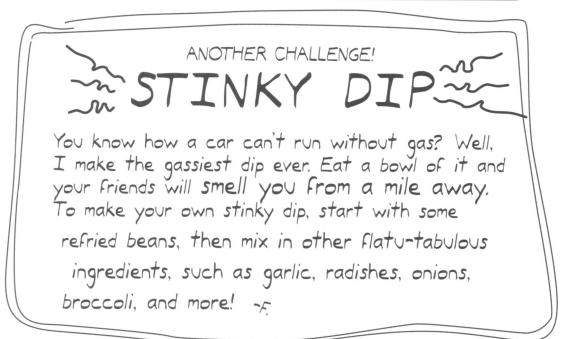

ANOTHER CHALLENGE!

## STINKY DIP

You know how a car can't run without gas? Well, I make the gassiest dip ever. Eat a bowl of it and your friends will **smell** you from a mile away. To make your own stinky dip, start with some refried beans, then mix in other flatu-tabulous ingredients, such as garlic, radishes, onions, broccoli, and more! -F.

## CHALLENGE 6

# Wake Up and Smell the Gloppy!

When it comes to concoctions, your nose can't always trust your eyes. Something might *look* beautiful but actually *smell* horrible. The opposite is true, too: A yucky-looking, barf-worthy mixture can actually have a lovely aroma. Your challenge: Make a mixture that looks positively gross—but is a feast for your nostrils. Using only stuff from your kitchen, mix together ingredients that look like they might be right at home in a swamp. Then, to give your concoction sneaky "smell-appeal," add some good-smelling ingredients, like a small amount of vanilla, peppermint, or almond extract (available in the baking aisle at the supermarket). Adding some cocoa powder is another strategy. Test your work by blindfolding another mad scientist and having them smell your concoction. If they say it smells like something they would eat, you've succeeded! But don't let them actually taste it.

## CHALLENGE 7

# Don't Tell Your Dentist!

Your sweet tooth will love this one. Your goal is to take a scoop of vanilla ice cream and mix in a *whole bunch* of sweet treats. Some suggestions: mini chocolate chips, mini marshmallows, M&M's, chocolate-covered pretzels, gummi bears. Then taste it! For extra messy fun: Taste your concoction without using a spoon. Just stick your face in the bowl and gobble it up. You might just need a shower.

# Glossary

**acidic solution** a substance that has an excess of hydrogen ions (H+). Examples: lemon juice, vinegar, and hydrochloric acid (such as the acid inside your stomach).

**atom** the tiniest particle of an element. Atoms are made of even smaller parts called protons, neutrons, and electrons.

**basic solution** a substance that has an excess of hydroxide ions (OH-). Examples: ammonia, toothpaste, and soap. Another word for a base is an *alkali*.

**chemical change** a change in which substances change into different substances. During a chemical change, bonds are broken and reformed between atoms. Examples: paper being burned, digesting food, dynamite exploding, and metal rusting. Compare to a *physical change*.

**chemistry** the science of what stuff is made of, and how different chemicals react together.

**colloid** a mixture that has tiny particles in it that don't dissolve into the solution. The molecules of a colloid are not fully combined. Examples: whipped cream, butter, jelly, paint, milk, gelatin, glue, and mayonnaise.

COCKAMAMIE describes something ridiculous or incredible, like my being fired from cowriting this book...

**concoction** a mixture of ingredients that is often the result of an experiment.

**density** a property of matter that describes how closely packed a material is (or as chemists say, its mass divided by its volume). Objects that are denser than others are heavier. A brick made out of gold is much more dense than a same size brick made out of Styrofoam.

And, you, Jordan, are a pretty good example of a dense guy compared to moi.

You didn't know I was so fluent in French, did you?

**electron** a tiny particle of an atom that orbits around the nucleus. All atoms have electrons spinning around at different distances from the nucleus. A hydrogen atom has one electron, and an atom of gold contains 79 electrons.

**element** a chemical that is made of only one type of atom. Examples: hydrogen, oxygen, gold, silver, lead, iron, and chlorine.

FLATULENCE intestinal gas that is released from inside the butt; commonly known as a fart. Sometimes loud, sometimes silent, and (I don't mean to brag) sometimes musical!

**hypothesis** a prediction in an experiment; an educated guess that can be tested to confirm or disprove it. Example: My hypothesis is that adding honey to my bubble soap solution will make longer-lasting bubbles.

And my hypothesis is that you are

going to send me

boatloads of money in gratitude, or else... or else... nah, better leave it a surprise.

**intermolecular forces** the electromagnetic forces that hold molecules together, which require energy, such as heat, to pull apart. The stronger the attraction between molecules, the more difficult it is to separate them.

**matter** any substance that has mass and takes up space; made of tiny particles called atoms; on Earth, usually a solid, liquid, or gas.

**molecule** the tiniest part of an element or compound that has the chemical properties of that substance. A molecule of water is two atoms of hydrogen linked with one atom of oxygen.

**nonpolar molecule** a molecule that does not have an electric charge at either end because the electrons are evenly distributed. Examples: vegetable oil and gasoline. Nonpolar materials do not dissolve polar materials.

**physical change** a change in which a material keeps its original chemical properties. Examples: breaking a pencil in half or melting an ice cube. Compare to a *chemical change*.

**polar molecule** a molecule that has a positive charge on one end and negative charge on the other. The side with more electrons has a negative charge; the side with fewer electrons has a positive charge. Polar materials only dissolve other polar materials.

**polymer** a material that is made of long chains of the same kind of molecule. Examples: Silly Putty, Jell-O, rubber bands, chewing gum, hair, nails, and DNA.

**scientific method** a careful, step-by-step way to search for answers to questions or problems. Steps include making observations, stating a hypothesis, collecting data to prove or disprove the hypothesis, and drawing a conclusion.

TARRADIDDLE a small lie, a fib, like when Jordan says my practical jokes aren't funny.

**viscosity** how easily a liquid flows—or doesn't. For example, honey has a greater viscosity than water does because it pours more slowly.

# Index

What do you get when you combine Jordan with $O_2$?

(An oxymoron!!)

What's brown and sticky?

(A stick.)

$E=MC^{Z}3$

So close, Albert; so close.

Ways to Get Revenge on Jordan
- Mess up his precious book.
- Dye his hair purple.
- Spread vicious rumors about his singing.

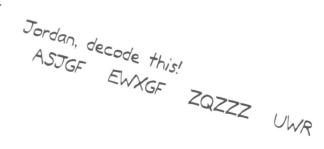

Jordan, decode this!
ASJGF    EWXGF    ZQZZZ    UWR

Gravity is a real downer!

This sentense has three erors.

Pranks for the memories, Jordan!!

Time Flies like an arrow. Fruit Flies like a banana.

What do you get when you combine Jordan with $O_2$?

(An oxymoron!!)

What's brown and sticky?

(A stick.)

$E=MC^{2}3$

So close, Albert; so close.

Ways to Get Revenge on Jordan
✓ • Mess up his precious book.
   • Dye his hair purple.
   • Spread vicious rumors about his singing.

Jordan, decode this!
ASJGF   EWXGF   ZQZZZ   UWR

Gravity is a real downer!

This sentence has three erors.

Pranks for the memories, Jordan!!

Time Flies like an arrow. Fruit flies like a banana.